D1809415

# Zits, Tits & Boys' Bits

# Zits, Tits & Boys' Bits

A guide to help the teenage boy
avoid life's little %^&#-ups

## Suzanne and Vernon Crew

### Illustrations by Miles Harper

www.alysbooks.com

## About the Authors

Sue and Vern are your average couple with seven children aged 6 to 36, a healthy curiosity about love, life, wine and whisky, and a firm belief that open and frank communication is the basis for a wonderful marriage and an inclusive family. They feel they do pretty well in this regard. Especially with the whisky.

Vern is an educator and applied linguist and has survived teaching, academe and administration in primary schools, colleges and higher education institutions around the world. After 10 years or so working in federal politics Sue now works in higher education as a policy advisor. Both share a love of language, a passion for their field, a devotion to their family, a ludicrous sense of humour and a lifetime commitment to each other.

Copyright © 2013
All rights reserved by Suzanne and Vernon Crew.

Aly's Books
PO Box 25
Kingsville Vic 3012
Australia
www.alysbooks.com

No part of this book may be reproduced or transmitted in any form or by any means, graphic, electronic, or mechanical, including photocopying, recording, taping, or by any information storage retrieval system, without the permission, in writing, from the publisher.

Book Design/Layout by Simone Hill.

ISBN: 978-0-9875296-2-6

**To our boys...**

*Ben, the advice I wish I could have given you years ago*
*Sam, to guide you now and in the years to come*
*Ali and Seb, for your future*

## To parents and caregivers from the authors...

This was a work of love for us, but we also saw it as a necessity. We wrote it for one of our boys as he reached adolescence. It was, and is, an intensely personal set of thoughts and advice. Having said that, enough of our friends, family and colleagues have read it and asked us to put together a generically publishable version for their sons, grandsons and, surprisingly, partners that we decided to give it a try.

In places the content and advice might be a little too close to the bone for some, but we do stress that we've aimed this book at those who aren't afraid to face what can sometimes be uncomfortable truths about adolescence for boys.

**Warning:** Contains teen/adult themes. 13 years and over recommended.

## To the teenage boy...

People, some well-meaning, some maybe not, have probably already started to give you basic instruction on life – 'Treat girls right', 'Be a man', 'Grow some balls', 'You'll be right' – but we bet very few people bother to explain what these clichés mean.

So this is what we want to do – give you a guide to what it means to be a good friend, good boyfriend and, in time, a good lover in every sense of the word.

Some of these things you may have already talked about with family or friends or probably will talk about at some time, but others are best left to the written word to avoid embarrassment on both sides.

Some of these things we know from bitter and sweet personal experience, others are the result of the collective wisdom of friends, both men and women, whom we respect and love.

Some of it you may not be ready for right now and you'll probably return to it later in life. The intention is that this is a kind of reference book that you can take from as you need it.

Don't tear yourself apart if you stuff up occasionally. We can't all be perfect all the time, but we hope that this guide will provide you with a good grounding that you can refer to time and time again.

You have enormous potential to be a man that the world admires. We hope that this book will give you a head start.

# WHAT IT'S ALL ABOUT

# LIFE IN GENERAL – BORING STUFF THAT MATTERS

**01** Although you probably don't believe it, your parents do understand your need to be cool – they've been there, done that, when they were your age. Really. No – really. Most parents would never want to interfere with your coolness, although threatening to do so is sometimes worth it for the entertainment value they get from your reaction.

**02** A desire for maximum coolness is scientifically proven to interfere with teenage boys being able to properly assess risk. Common sense doesn't kick in again until age 25 for most males. Some men reach old age without any obvious improvement…

**03** When parents do seriously say "No!" to an activity where they honestly believe your desire for coolness is interfering with your ability to assess risk, no amount of teen-mood will change their minds. It's for the best. Try to remember this when you're plotting revenge behind their backs!

**04** **Be open to new experiences and new people.**

**05** Prioritise travel. Each new adventure will change you, shape you and develop you into a citizen of the world – even the inevitable dodgy experiences in cheap bars and backpackers' hostels.

**06** It's easy to stereotype people by age, race, sex, sexuality, class and religion, or a combination of these, but try not to. If people were honest about this, they'd admit that it's something that they struggle with. We all stereotype at some level, but fight it as much as possible. By giving in to stereotypes we narrow our view of the world.

**07** Intelligence and respect for others are nothing to do with gender. Because you're male, it doesn't mean that you're always right, or that you can ignore or rubbish someone's view or opinion just because they're female and/or you disagree with them. If you disagree about something, have a reasoned conversation about it, don't try to dominate.

**08** We know that boys generally aren't great readers, but it's REALLY important to have some basic knowledge about 'life in general' – what's happening on the news, a bit of basic history, the odd bit of literature, latest trends. Men that can only talk about the footy or how good their last crap was are boring. Believe us, there are a lot of them out there.

**09** Your word really is your bond and if you give someone your word that you'll do something, you have to do whatever it is you've promised. Keeping your word is something that gains you respect from others. If you don't keep your word, no-one respects you – it's as simple as that.

**10** If you're wrong about something, admit it and apologise honestly and sincerely, preferably straightaway. If you do, you'll get respect. Amazingly, heaps of adults have never got their head around this, which is why the workforce is full of arse-coverers. Plonkers all!

**11** Never lie. It's easier to be truthful (you don't have to try to remember what you've said before) and anyway people are generally very good at knowing when you're lying, even if they don't call you on it.

**12** Everyone, including you, has a little voice inside that tells them what's right – it doesn't mean you're bonkers, it's your conscience talking. Always listen to it and not to other people who may be trying to persuade you to do something that deep down you know isn't right. Often that little voice may be difficult to hear because of other people's views, temptations and pressures, but always make the effort to ask yourself what the right thing to do is – and listen to the answer. It may just be a slight feeling of unease at what you're proposing to do but that's enough – it means 'No!'

**13** Accepting criticism is something everyone finds hard, especially when their self esteem is a bit low. Some criticism is intended to hurt and crush, while other forms of criticism are intended to help you grow. Learning the difference between the two can be painful, but if you immediately become agitated you won't learn to tell the difference between the good and the bad. The best thing to do is say "Thanks. I'll think about that," go away, calm down and do just that – think about it. If the criticism aligns with your little voice within (see previous tip) you should take it on board. If not, disregard it.

**14** A lot of boys are brought up to hide their feelings, never show when they're hurt, never admit they're worried or have a problem etc. In fact, that's really bad for you and the best thing you can do is to tell someone you trust about your problem or hurt. They may be able to help you fix it, but even if they can't, you'll feel better for having shared your problem with someone sympathetic, 'on your side' and who'll give you an honest opinion and advice. People you love and who love you are best for this.

**15** You may think that because you're quiet and not very extroverted, you're unusual. Not so – in fact the vast majority of people are introverts, but they learn to cover it up by pretending to be confident. They're not really anywhere near as confident as they'd like you to believe.

**16** Eyes are the most revealing part of the body and can tell you pretty much everything about how someone is feeling, or about how they're trying to hide what they're feeling.

**17** Boys tend to brag more than girls, so discount a lot of what boys say they've done or achieved.

**18** **Don't gossip. Words wound just as much as actions.**

**19** Similarly, don't voice your negative opinions about other people in public. It reveals more to others about your own prejudices than you think.

**20** The qualities you like or admire in other people are those you like or admire in yourself. On the other hand, the qualities you dislike in other people are those you dislike in yourself. Consider this before criticising others.

**21** Everyone makes decisions based on the information and circumstances that they're aware of at the time. No-one deliberately makes poor or bad decisions. If a decision you make turns out later to be one you're not happy with, don't beat yourself up, just accept that you made the best decision you could at the time, correct it if you can, and move on. If you can't correct it, don't worry, see what you can learn from the experience and remember it for next time – just don't get hung up on it.

**22** Comedian George Caitlin once said that fighting for peace is like screwing for virginity. In other words, it's a pointless exercise. It's usually possible to see or sense when a fight is about to erupt and then to slip away as quickly and quietly as possible so that you don't draw attention to yourself.

**23** There are two situations in which you may not be able to get out of a fight – if you're caught in the middle of a brawl, or if someone starts to pick on you. If you need to defend yourself, aim for vulnerable spots like the eyes and balls. If the other person has a weapon (a knife, glass etc.) – don't hang around, just run. Look for a group of people to join. You're less likely to be attacked in front of witnesses.

**24** **It doesn't matter what century it is – the saying 'Manners maketh man' is as true today as it was hundreds of years ago. Like it or not, as a child/teenager all adults judge you by your manners and once you're an adult, other adults will too.**

**25** Some so-called 'old-fashioned' manners are probably not necessary these days e.g. always walking next to the curb so the girl doesn't get splashed by cars going through puddles, or standing when a lady enters or leaves the room. Some girls can be a little touchy about you opening a door and/or pulling out their seat for them. Others love it. You'll need to suss this out for yourself. However, you should try and remember the basics. The following are essential, especially if you want to impress the chick of your dreams:

- Don't grunt greetings
- Use please, thank you and excuse me
- Wait until everyone's ready before starting to take food or eat
- Know how to use a knife and fork properly
- Don't speak with your mouth full
- Never take the last piece of food without asking first
- Stand up for women and the elderly on public transport
- Let people enter a shop or room before you leave.

# SCHOOL – NO, YOU REALLY DO NEED TO READ THIS BIT!

## 26  Time management and consistent effort is more important than a big brain.

**27** Always start the school year well and make a good impression early on. Once a teacher thinks you're a hard worker, they're more likely to forgive the odd poor assignment. If they think you're a general slacker, they'll judge everything you say and do accordingly.

**28** If you want to blend into the classroom without being noticed too much, don't sit at the back and don't sit at the front. Teachers assume that children sitting at the back are lazy and/or troublesome; equally children at the front are seen as eager beavers who can be relied on to answer questions.

**29** Over the years you'll come across teachers that are good, bad and indifferent. It's easy to work hard in the classes you like, but much harder when you're stuck listening to some old bastard with a bad temper. The thing to remember is no matter how bad they are, they have information and skills that you need. You need to use teachers like this, you don't have to like them. Anyway, there can be a perverse, up-yours kind of pleasure in doing well in class in spite of that miserable old windbag!

**30** Try not to freak out about essays and reports, however hard the assignment might seem at first. If you know the basic format for the answer (Google it if your teacher hasn't given away the secret) you can't go wrong. The right format with some basic research should get you a decent pass.

**31** Learn to reference early on – it shows that you know your stuff and it's not that hard. It'll save you heaps of time both at school and well into university, if that's where you're headed.

**32** Revise your lessons each afternoon if you can – even 5 to 10 minutes will help some of it stick in your brain.

**33** **Don't believe other kids if they say they aren't doing any work. If they're doing well they're working hard, no matter how brainy they are. It's often not cool to admit to hard work, so many students do it secretly.**

**34** **Class jokers may seem cool and funny at first, but if their jokes are continually at the expense of other kids and teachers, they're usually regarded as tossers before long.**

**35** Kids who know you at school will remember you and judge you on your current behaviour, even as an adult – sad but true. You'll do that to them, too.

# FAMILY
# AND FRIENDS

**36** The saying – You can choose your friends but not your family – is true. Sorry, but you're stuck for life with the family you've got!

**37** Your family will love you no matter what you do – even if it's something you think they'll disapprove of. They might not like what you've done, but they'll ALWAYS be there to support you.

**38** You'll probably go through a phase during which you'll find everything about your parents utterly embarrassing. Try not to make a big thing out of it. While your parents do understand, it's best to talk about mutual expectations rather than suddenly shunning them.

**39** Don't be super-critical or mocking of your siblings all the time, however much fun this might be – they may not say anything, but deep down they'll be very hurt.

**40** Make up your own mind about people, don't be swayed by school-ground opinion on others. This tends to change with the wind and isn't worth worrying about.

**41** Always stand up for your friends – even when they're being dicks. However, if one of your friends is being really stupid or hurtful to others, don't be afraid to tell them what you think of them. Even if they don't appreciate it at the time, you're actually doing them a favour.

**42** You find out who your real friends are when you're in trouble. They're easy to identify – they stand by you and aren't afraid to tell you when you're being the aforementioned dick.

**43** **Remember who your friends are. Don't try to be one of the 'cool' kids at the cost of your true friendships.**

**44** Even when families live apart all over the world, they can still be very close and love one another just as much as much as ever. It takes effort to keep these bonds alive, but it's well worth it.

**45** Family can still keep an eye on you from far away these days, thanks to Facebook and other social networks!

**46** Look after your sister/s and female friends and make sure that other boys/men treat them well.

**47** Grandparents can be annoying sometimes. However, they love you dearly and should always be respected. Most people don't realise how important their grandparents are to them until they're gone, so don't be one of those people who rejects their grandparents' love and knowledge – they've lived a long time and they know a whole lot of amazing STUFF.

**48** If you're given a gift that you don't like (oddly enough, family members can be the worst at this), don't let it show – be polite and thank whoever gave it to you. If you decide to junk the gift later, make sure that the giver doesn't know that you've done that – it's very hurtful. If someone persists in giving you gifts that you hate, find opportunities during the year to let them know the sort of thing you like.

**49** Chores and helpfulness – you get huge credit for volunteering to help with chores, tidying or other jobs around the house, rather than having to be asked. If you have to be asked or chased every time, parents get sick of asking, you get sick of being nagged – everyone gets grumpy – and you don't get as much pocket money!

**50** Avoid the temptation to share family gossip or general weirdness with outsiders just for fun. Most families are a little odd in some ways, but family nuttiness should stay in the family.

# WHAT'S THAT ON MY FACE – A VOLCANO?

**51** Zits are a fact of life as a teenager, but you can help keep them at bay by washing your face twice daily with the face wash your parents probably buy you in vain. You don't have to tell your mates you're doing this, of course. Very few teenagers escape having zits naturally, so it's very likely that anyone your age with permanently clear skin is using medicated face wash anyway and hoping no-one finds out.

**52** **However tempting it may be, don't squeeze zits, at least not until the whitehead emerges, otherwise they leave messy scars later on.**

**53** It's not girly to take care of yourself!

**54** Teenage boy smell exists. Memories of catching the school bus in the afternoons, overwhelmed by the stench of it, still haunt most women! It's caused mainly by testosterone, which is huge in your body during your teenage years so you can't get rid of it entirely, but washing well (use soap or shower gel – don't just let the water run over you), washing your hair daily, changing underwear and socks often and using deodorant will help.

**55** Talking of smells – be sparing with deodorant and aftershave. Yes, you need deodorant, but go easy if it's a powerfully scented variety. Be even more sparing with aftershave. Generally, if you use both, use an unscented deodorant.

**56** Shaving – it'll take a few years before your beard matures enough for you to carry off the designer stubble look, and your school probably won't let you grow a beard or moustache anyway, so do shave regularly. And, yes, sometimes you'll shave the head off a zit and it'll hurt. A lot.

**57** Generally, women don't like hairy backs or cracks. If it bothers you – wax! Yes, it'll hurt at the time, but in the long run it'll be well worth it in terms of chick-approval.

**58** **Don't worry, your penis IS big enough – but keep it clean!**

**59** **Iron your clothes before a date – it makes an impression. If you don't, it won't matter how clean your penis is, you'll never get to use it.**

**60** Don't try to iron your clothes while you're wearing them. We know that sounds like common sense, but you'd be surprised how many people have burned themselves thinking they'd save time ironing their clothes that way.

# GIRLS – WHAT ARE THEY ABOUT?

**61** No matter how hard you try, you will never fully understand girls or women, but you have to give it a go. Girls and women think men are impossible to understand, so both sexes firmly believe that they are uncomplicated and that it's only the other sex that's weird.

**62** Always treat girls you like, either romantically or as friends, like ladies. Do this even if you don't like them. This means no farting, burping, swearing, smutty remarks, dirty jokes or references to private parts – yours or theirs. While most girls put up with this behaviour, they don't like it.

**63** **If you're in love, never be afraid to say it and show it every day. Love breeds love. Respect breeds respect – the best circle of all to get into.**

**64** Girls like gifts, even if they say they don't. The best gifts are those that come as a surprise. The value isn't important, but the sentiment is.

**65** You can't go wrong with flowers – girls of all ages love getting flowers (unless flowers give them hay fever – better check that first).

**66** **The 'F' word – no, not that one, the other one – "Fine!" If a girl or woman says that to you she may well mean the opposite, and if you persist in whatever it was you were doing or wanted to do, you'll be in deep trouble.**

**67** If your girlfriend says "Do what you want" – for goodness sake, DON'T do what you want – it will probably be disastrous. She really wants you to do what she wants. Be wary if this becomes a constant pattern of behaviour, though. If it does, you may want to re-think your choice of girlfriend.

**68** Always be courteous and treat girls well (yes, including your sister/s), even when you've known them for ages – it will pay off because many blokes don't have the maturity and sense to do this.

**69** Be interested in what girls are telling you (yes, even if it's boring or weird girly stuff). If a girl trusts you with what's on her mind, it's a great compliment and you should value it. If she really does bore you stupid with her prattle, she's not the right girl for you, so be courteous, listen attentively and respond appropriately, then move on as gently as possible. That way you still get bonus points with the girl community for being nice, and anyway you should never put someone down or be cruel about what they have to say.

**70** Girls don't understand when boys have something on their minds, but don't want to talk about it.

**71** **Girls have very good memories and don't ever forget any bad things you may have done. They may forgive you, but they don't forget.**

**72** Girls are forever worried about their body shape and whether they look OK. Always be supportive and find something genuinely positive to say unless whatever they're wearing is an absolute disaster, in which case find a nice way to say so without reducing them to tears.

**73** The answer to the question you're bound to get asked a lot during your life, "Does my bum look big in this?" – is always, without exception, "NO!"

**74** Girls spend a lot of time trying to get their look just right. They take into account details that most blokes never consider, like matching their eye colour with their dress, shoes or some accessory. If you train yourself to notice that kind of thing and can comment well on it, they like it a lot and will think of you as understanding, sensitive, possibly bonkable...

**75** ALWAYS try to notice a girl's haircut and if she changes it compliment her even if it looks awful. If her new hairstyle is a bad one, she knows it anyway and the last thing she wants you to do is reinforce her unhappiness with the new look. Your job – not an easy one – is to say something that will reassure her that people aren't going to fall about laughing when she goes out with her new hairstyle, but not to be so enthusiastic about it that she knows you're lying or may think it really does look good. Listen to what her girlfriends say when they comment on her new look, it may give you ideas.

**76** Be careful about comparing your girlfriend's look or personality with others. You might be able to get away with comparing her with some glamorous movie or TV star, but definitely not with one of her friends – that might lead her to suspect that you like her friend more than her.

**77** **Compliments – keep it real. Girls know when you're just saying something and don't mean it. It's a fine line, but there is one. It might take you a while to suss this out.**

**78** Girls need to talk and don't understand that boys often prefer not to. Girls use talking to get to know other people better, to maintain relationships, to offload problems (no, they don't always expect you to fix whatever the problem is, they often just want you to listen) – all sorts of reasons that don't necessarily make sense to boys. Talking makes them feel better and they may say all sorts of things that may seem hurtful, but often they're just letting off steam. So keep calm, learn to listen (with all your attention, don't watch TV or play with your computer while she's talking to you) and discount any hurtful stuff. You can find out whether she really meant the hurtful stuff when it's all over and you're both calm.

**79** Eyes are very revealing. Many girls think that what might make them attractive to a boy they like is showing a lot of leg, or boobage. Actually, the most reliable indicator of whether someone is interested in you is whether they make eye contact for just a fraction longer than they need to. This applies to boys and girls, so if you want to show a girl you're interested, do the eye contact and slight smile thing, not the stupid blokey show-offy thing, which turns them off. Similarly, with girls, register the eye contact they make with you, not any excessive skin they may be flashing – you get a nicer class of girl that way, too.

# OMG – SHE LIKES ME!

**80** It may seem to you that many girls, particularly when they're still learning about boys, romance and love, seem to prefer boys who are louder and generally more in your face, rather than quieter, gentler boys. You may find this difficult to believe right now, but most girls that you wish would be interested in you will realise after a while that the sort of boy they're really looking for is like you. Be patient – they'll come to you in time.

**81** **Yes, a girl can be your best friend. Sex doesn't have to be what it's all about with every girl you know. On the other hand, if you and a girl are not only good friends and have the same sense of humour and values, but are also interested in each other romantically and sexually, that's just about the best combination you could ever wish for.**

**82** Take it easy with a new relationship. In time it may become true lurve, but if you start declaring undying love and devotion too soon it's very likely the girl will run a mile.

**83** Never tell a girl you love her in an attempt to get into her pants – tempting, we know, but, well, just don't do it. There'll be too many hurt feelings and you'll get a bad reputation. If you're lucky you might find a 'friend with benefits' instead – much less complicated!

**84** Try not to confuse love with lust or infatuation. Lust is when you desperately want to have sex with a girl even though you might not like her much or know her that well. It's a pure physical yearning. Infatuation can lead to love, but this is rare. Infatuation is often a one-way obsession in which you can't see any faults or flaws in the other person and although it can be powerful for a while, it doesn't usually last very long.

**85** Flirting can be fun, but if you're already in a relationship it can be very hurtful for your girlfriend. Some girlfriends don't mind if you flirt, but if you're going to do that you need to have discussed it with her first and agreed how far you can go so that it doesn't become hurtful and destroy the relationship.

**86** 'Playing away' i.e. having short-term affairs or one night stands when you're away from home or when your girlfriend is away. Don't. It may be exciting or tempting on occasion, but it's dishonest, dishonourable, insulting to your girlfriend, it will become known to her and everyone else, it's dangerous health-wise for you and your existing girlfriend (you don't know the new girl's sexual history) and do you really want to go with the sort of girl who'd let you have sex with her on a one night stand basis? OK, don't answer that.

**87** In general, it seems to be true that if a girl has been in love with you, but then falls out of love with you and dumps you – that's it. There's no coming back from that, so don't waste time and effort trying to get her back. Move on.

**88** You probably don't believe this now, but it's true that love is a spiritual thing. Sex in a loving relationship is a whole lot better than casual sex – it's a spiritual thing in itself. Until you feel it yourself, it's hard to describe, but it does exist. If you have any doubts, it's not IT. Don't settle for second best.

# BEER O'CLOCK

**89** Drinking games are a rite of passage – they can be dangerous, but are fun if you remember to show some balls (not literally!) and pull out before it gets stupid or dangerous. Better to take some stick from your mates in the short-term than have your stomach pumped in hospital – very messy, painful and more than a tad embarrassing.

**90** Look out for your friends , both male and female, when drinking and know the signs of alcohol poisoning (confusion, passed out or cannot be woken, vomiting, fits or seizures, slow breathing – fewer than eight breaths per minute – or irregular breathing, low body temperature, bluish skin colour or paleness). It's better to call an ambulance than to try to deal with it yourself. Don't worry that they'll be in trouble the next day with their parents – at least they'll be alive.

**91** **NEVER, NEVER, NEVER get into a car driven by anyone who's had even a couple of drinks, a joint or any other drugs. Call a taxi or your parents, or walk with a group of friends – anything other than getting into a vehicle with a drunk or drugged driver!**

**92** Learn to know your limits, but this takes time. Until you figure this out for yourself, if you feel you're beginning to slur your words or if you feel you have to take extra care to walk steadily, STOP DRINKING for a while. Go for a walk in the fresh air to clear your head. Any excuse will do e.g. toilet break, headache, need to make phone call/answer phone. If possible, have a glass of water.

**93** Mixing your drinks is never a good idea, particularly if drinking 'shots' is involved. The hangover next day is dreadful.

**94** 'Shouts' are bad news when you've reached your limit, but are inevitable in the Australian culture and can be a good thing in the right circumstances. Never miss out on your shout even if you're a bit behind and haven't finished your own drink yet. If you're really starting to get plastered and your round isn't due yet, leave cash on the table for your mates before packing it in. Other blokes never forgive you for missing your shout.

**95** It's pretty foul to throw-up and start drinking again. Not a good look if you're out on the pull.

**96** **Eating is not cheating. It's common sense to have something in your stomach to soak up the alcohol. A large glass of water before you start on the beer can also help.**

**97** Unfortunately, some people become aggressive when drinking – you can't always tell who'll be affected in this way. Sometimes your quietest, shyest friends turn into rabid madmen after two beers. If they're a good friend, be aware of this and learn to avoid their bad behaviour triggers. Or just keep away from them when they've been drinking.

**98** Smoking – tobacco, that is. You'll have been deluged with advice, ads etc. telling you that smoking is massively addictive, seriously bad for you and will shorten your life drastically, but you may still feel pressure to try it because your mates are doing it. Don't. What the ads say is true and smoking leads to some truly awful ways to die.

**99** We can't give you a lot of advice on drugs, never having been into this much ourselves, but from watching others, paranoia (massive suspicion of others, becoming obsessive over certain things) is a real problem with some common drugs. We've also had some friends who tended to wet themselves when using drugs – never a good look.

# AT LAST, THE BIT YOU WERE WAITING FOR – SEX (INCLUDING SELF-HELP...)

**100** Sometimes it will seem as though your penis has a mind of its own and you'll get erections at embarrassing moments. This is normal during your teen years and, yes, girls do notice and find it funny or yucky depending on how they feel about you and about sex generally. If you're really lucky they may take it as a compliment, but that's not something you should rely on.

**101** There's nothing wrong with masturbating – after all, it's a lot of fun and it's free! It's perfectly normal and pretty much everyone (yes, including girls) does or has done it, unless they're a bit weird. It won't do you any harm at all, but it should be a private activity.

**102** If you masturbate in bed, use a tissue to catch your stuff and flush it down the toilet – don't just throw the used tissue in your rubbish bin. Your Mum shouldn't have to wash your crinkly, smelly sheets or pyjamas or empty a rubbish bin containing dodgy tissues. Similarly with 'wet dreams'. It's quite common – and normal – for teenage boys to wake up during the night feeling a bit sticky and discover that they've 'come' in their sleep. Nothing to worry about, just clean it up.

**103** Never masturbate in the bath unless you're willing to clean it up afterwards – your stuff floats and creates a gooey, sticky mess.

**104** **Girls like sex too. They may not say so, but they're just as interested in it as you are. They have more to lose, though – they might get pregnant, they might get a reputation as 'easy', a slut etc. – so they may well be less casual in their attitudes towards sex than many boys.**

**105** Virginity is more important to most girls than it is to boys and it's a big thing for them to decide they want to have full-on sex with a boy. If you're lucky enough to have this happen to you, make sure you respect the girl's decision and her, especially afterwards.

**106** Again, if you 'get lucky', don't tell anyone – it's just between the two of you. The only exception to this is your Mum! (Yeah, right – you can probably tell a Mum wrote that last bit.)

**107** Your first time may not be as wonderful as you'd expected, either for you or your partner. That's absolutely normal. Being good at sex is something you learn with practice and experience – and that's something that virgins don't yet have. So relax and enjoy the learning curve.

**108** Girls take longer to 'warm up' than boys do, so don't rush it when you're having a sexual encounter with a girl. Take your time, be sure she's ready and willing to take whatever the next step is – and it will work much better for you both than if you try to go too far too fast.

**109** **Time spent on foreplay is time very well spent. If you don't know what foreplay is, Google it and find out.**

**110** Girls have many erogenous zones – bits of their bodies that feel good when stroked or kissed – pretty much all over them, not just their nipples and genitals (though see warning in next point). You have only one erogenous zone. You know where it is. Go figure. Work with that.

**111** Girls really like being stroked and kissed and in general like to be touched more gently than boys. This applies particularly to their breasts, nipples and genitals, so don't be rough, and don't pinch or squeeze. Your girlfriend may want to take it slowly, so don't try to touch places that she doesn't want touched.

**112** Learning to undo a bra strap with one hand without interrupting the action is a skill well worth perfecting. Practice on a huge teddy bear if you can find one (maybe a sister's?)!

**113** Don't be surprised if you find the occasional nipple hair on a girl. Most girls pluck them out, but you might come across one who's obviously not keen to use tweezers. If so, it's definitely not the done thing to express surprise, for example, "Holy shit, furry tits!"

**114** Pubes! In the good old days, EVERYONE had them. These days, not so much, for either sex. Don't be fooled by the urban myth that pubes are dirty and disgusting. They're not. They're designed to keep everything clean. However, in recent years it's become fashionable to do away with pubes. If you choose to keep your pubes, always keep them tidy – no one likes to have to spit one out in the middle of a sexual encounter. If you choose to remove them, use depilatory cream or wax, NEVER a razor and don't use hair removal cream immediately after sex. It stings!

**115** Yes, pubes do come in different colours, usually but not always the natural colour of people's head hair. Girls have a habit of messing with their hair colour, which can be a bit confusing...

**116** It's common for people of both genders to have 'unbalanced' bits of their bodies – girls usually have one boob a little bigger than the other and boys nearly always have one testicle that hangs lower than the other. Testicles can also appear to move up or down on their own, which can freak girls (and boys) out, though actually it's just a reaction to temperature, sexual excitement, fear, lots of things.

**117** Girls have a clitoris, which is a lot like your penis except much smaller. It's often hidden in the folds of a girl's 'lady's bits', until she gets aroused sexually. Then it grows, just like your penis, becoming erect but nowhere near as big. The clitoris is very sensitive, so be very gentle with it – if you are, the girl will like it a lot.

**118** If a girl says "No!" or "Stop!" she means it. You need to listen, no matter how excited you are, and stop whatever it is you're doing.

**119** **When it's over for you (i.e. when you've 'come'), it's not necessarily over for the girl, so keep going and think of her pleasure, not yours. You'll be able to tell when she's 'come' – although see the next point...**

**120** Girls have one great advantage over boys when it comes to sex – if the circumstances are right (meaning if you've done your job well) they can have multiple orgasms in quick succession, while you need a bit of time to recover before you can perform again. Yes, we know, not fair…

**121** No girl in the history of the world has ever found 'dry-humping' her leg a turn-on.

**122** **Always use protection (condoms) when you have sex, at least until you're in a long-term relationship, trust each other completely, know each other's sexual history and have made a decision together about what you're going to do about contraception.**

**123** Learning to use a condom is a skill you'll need to perfect. Practice putting one on yourself in the privacy of your room. If that's too gross, practice on a banana. You need to squeeze the nipply bit on the end to get the air out of it and then (still squeezing the nipply bit) roll the rest of it down over the full length of your penis.

**124** Taking a condom off without spilling the contents is also a skill – and one it's really important to get right, otherwise sperm can escape and an unwanted pregnancy may well result. Take it off while your penis is still erect and hold it at the base so it doesn't slip off when you pull out. Then dispose of it discreetly somewhere appropriate i.e. tie a knot in it so your stuff can't escape, wrap it in a tissue or plastic bag and put it in a bin. Best not to flush it down the toilet as it's not good environmentally and it can block the plumbing – never a good look…

**125** Girls tell their best friends pretty much everything about sex – the size of your penis, any weird sexual preferences, your status as a lover (good, bad, selfish or indifferent), the frequency of your requests for sex… the list goes on. This continues into woman-hood. Unlike men, it is not about exaggerating sexual prowess. On some weird level, not explainable to men, they find sex hilarious.

**126** Being gay or bisexual – Most people have times during their teenage years when they wonder whether or not they may be gay or bi. Almost everyone fantasises about homosexual or bi sex at times, but for most people this is as far as it goes. Some people experiment with this for a while, too – this isn't unusual, either. Some people then decide they're straight after all and move on with their lives. Some will decide they really are gay or bi and will move on with their lives in that direction. Whichever way it goes, it's OK as long as no-one is pressured into taking one way over the other.

**127** **At some point you'll come across pornography. The thing to remember about porn is that it's not real – the people in porn movies or video clips are usually acting out a script and may well be doing things that are extreme compared with the sexual experiences that most people engage in on a routine basis.**

**128** In a healthy sexual relationship, kinky sex may have its place but should never completely replace 'the basics' – after all, there's a very good reason why traditional sexual activities have remained popular for thousands of years i.e. they're damn good.

**129** Especially when young people are starting out on their sex lives, they're unlikely to be ready to do many of the things you might see porn actors doing. If you have expectations that your girlfriends will be ready and willing to do what porn actresses do, you'll almost certainly freak them out.

**130** Fantasising about what you (and your partner) might like to do sexually is normal and fun, but just be warned that if you try out your fantasies in real life they may not always live up to what you or your partner had hoped for.

**131** In real life most people's bodies aren't shaped like porn stars (e.g. huge boobs like melons or penises the size of a horse's) unless they've had cosmetic surgery. So try not to have unrealistic expectations of your own or your partners' bodies.

**132** **Don't take other guys' stories of sexual 'triumphs' at face value. They tend to exaggerate wildly.**

**133** Never share stories of any of your own sexual 'triumphs' – these stories get around and the girls you're talking about WILL get to hear them.

# IS THAT IT?

Well, yes and no. There's a lot more we could have included – but that's probably more than enough to get you started and on the way to manhood.

By the way, we certainly didn't get it right every time, your parents didn't either, and we don't expect that you will, but along the way we've learned a few things and we've tried to put them in this little book. The big thing is... in spite of life's ups and downs, it's brilliant, and it's the only one you'll ever have, so get out there, listen to the little voice inside that tells you what's right and give it your best shot.

Lightning Source UK Ltd.
Milton Keynes UK
UKIC02n2309271215
265419UK00002B/13